We must not linger

Kate Rose

MOSAÏQUEPRESS

Praise for
We must not linger
by Kate Rose

In these poems, Kate Rose occupies various positions
between 'stillness and surge', from quietly acute
observation of nature to the urgent sensuality of
poems such as 'In subzero temperatures'. Icy weather
is a consistent presence in the collection, reflected in
the poet's crisp clarity and spare but moving language.
Although there is a chill atmosphere in the settings,
there is also the warmth of deep emotional response to
people, region and landscape. These are poems that will
stay with you and ask to be read and re-read over time.

> **Derek Sellen**, *Canterbury Festival Poet of the
> Year 2018 and 2023, winner of Poets Meet
> Politics, O Bheal Five Words and Poetry Pulse*

'We must not linger' is in fact an invitation to do
exactly the opposite – to explore an in-between world
glistening with icy menace and superstition, blessed
with the rich colours of surprise jewels, glaucous
oceans, and the warmth of baking bread. The riddling
quality and haunting figures of these lyric poems
compel the reader to return to their intriguing shores –
to glimpse an elusive inner land- and sea-scape, where
past and present merge; and to savour deep moments
of beauty and light.

> **Sue Kindon**, *poet*

If this collection from Kate Rose was only bought for one poem, 'The night-time visitors of a dying country man', the reader would be satisfied. *Aren't you curious the dying man cries from an open window*, Kate asks her reader. Profound words belonging only to a thinking poet, and ending with the most beautiful of words, *A song thrush calls from the chestnut tree*. An excellent collection for those with a love of poetry.

John Eliot, *poet, editor, critic*

This collection will leave a mark, doused by moisture in all its forms: snow, ice, hoarfrost, rain, storm, tempest, tide, wave, spray, surf, foam, spit, cloud, fog, dew, tear, breath, blood, soup, mud, champagne, venom.
Lines are frozen, drank, dank, dipped, damp, wet, washed, wept, seeped, drenched, swollen, bobbing, afloat, overflowing.
From sea, ocean, depth, surge, shallow, shoreline, coastline, seaside, beachside, river, gorge, stream, pond, ditch, bucket, basin, bowl, jug, flute, blotter, dog mouth, kiss.
Linger beneath Kate's watering-can Rose as her poems flower, soak you in her lulling, draw you like water.

Karen Gemma Brewer, *poet, singer, actor*

First published in 2025

MOSAÏQUE PRESS
Registered office:
Bank Gallery
High Street
Kenilworth CV8 1LY

Cover illustration: *Snow over the valley* (oil on board)
Copyright © Nia MacKeown 2025

ISBN 978-1-906852-26-9

For Andrew

Contents

8   *Acknowledgements*

11   Beneath the surface

12   Evensong

13   Leonie takes a chance

14   Leaving the boat

15   The purity of first?

16   In subzero temperatures

17   No solace from rain

18   Truth

19   Beginning

20   Hope

21   Walking with ice

22   Bringing home the bread

23   It is enough

24   Journeying through

25   Morning crossing

26   The night-time visitors of a dying country man

27   Awakening 1

28   Awakening 2

29   Shucking oysters
30   Seaside observations
31   Mother's gaze
32   Instances of blue
33   Green Ribbon
34   Crossing the line
35   The falling of Gibson's mother
36   On receiving a brooch on her wedding day
      October 1946
37   Grief
38   Missing Signs

40   *About the author*
41   *About the illustrator*

'It is enough' and 'Truth' (titled 'Shells') first appeared
in *Correnti Incrociate 4* (Mosaïque Press, 2024)

Acknowledgements

SPECIAL THANKS to Treignac Stanza, Charente Writers, poetry@gouzon, Melanie More, René Shoemaker, and my editor and publisher, Chuck Grieve of Mosaïque Press, for his patience and encouragement.

BY THE SAME AUTHOR:
Brushstrokes (Mosaïque Press, 2022)
Whispers of the Tides (Premo from London, 2024)

The time will come
when, with elation,
you will greet yourself arriving
at your own door, in your own mirror,
and each will smile at the other's welcome

DEREK WALCOTT
from 'Love After Love'

Beneath the surface
(Robert Ryman 1930-2019)

In the afternoon gallery people enter, stop, saunter, stop.
In the gallery – shadows pass, then light.
Shadow. Shadow. Light.
His painting escapes through gaps,
reaches me,
pulls me
into its white. Its silence.
I can be still. I can be light.
I can swim beneath the surface and survive.
I can return to my ten-year-old self,
nose pushed against a window pane,
watching snow fill cracks between pebbles and grass.
Cover branches, trees, whole towns,
houses where no-one speaks.
I reach into snow. It absorbs my arms, hands, face,
hearing, sight.
I am snow.

Evensong

Was it here, in these chapel moments,
hands covering our faces,
hiding whispers that cut into night,

knees on bony ground, we murmured
'Our Father?'
The spit of candles.
Incensed breath.
Peeping into dreams.
Lovers in moments of light.

Light that covered trees and stars in outstretched arms.
Candlelight.
The breath of amen.
The heat of others.
Here was flesh. Blood.
Where fingers almost touched.

Leonie takes a chance

The slap cracks across the field. Leonie searches the horizon. Bare hills, the dolmen hidden by shadow. She strokes smooth conkers in her hankie. *She will add them to her collection.* She wants toast. Merri makes toast. Butter smothered. She needs Merri, damp arms, fleshy. She is never frightened at Merri's. Stuffed cats. A poppet. Wind chimes. She keeps her hands in her pockets. She will wait until the sisters walk on. Her face is hot. Red. Four fingers etched across her cheek. Merri told her she was unique. The sisters call it peculiar. She doesn't want to be. She reaches upwards, touches a golden leaf. Whispers fall. *Ears are funny things. So weird. So crucial.* She tastes their wayward words. Climbs the stile at the end of the field. The sisters call her name, pull her backwards. Her path ahead is brambled, twists into night. Merri will wait.

Leaving the boat

She called him Chicca. They lived at the bottom of a boat.
She feared water. She built a cage from peacock feathers,
backbones, firewood. She told him about hills, vines, tall
cedars, rows of olive trees, oil for roasting, mint with lemons.
His first word was freedom. He longed for dawn, for green,
moss, forest floors. On upper decks others prayed, counted
time, scolded dogs, rebuked rain grumbled at their women.
They threw Chicca to the moon. Then threw him again and
again, until his broken body brought back an olive branch.
He hooked it around her waist; pulled her southward through
thunder into open sky, until they brushed green treetops in a
cedar valley.

The purity of first?

He taught her to swim beach side.
Water was seaweed green
(emerald beneath the ocean).
Bottled, shadowed, weightless,
cold as a smile he once wore
(so verdant it drank her in).
He offered courage, a caress
a cave of memories.
Guiding her through storms as she swam new seas;
kept her body afloat through each new stroke.
His voice called from depths she'd never known;
chastising when she travelled out of reach;
invasive, like kelp twisting round her underbelly.

In subzero temperatures

In our dark place
where winter keeps us,
an oak burns.
Snow blocks our lane.
No robin sings; a hawk soars
above silver fields.

In these days, hours,
these leafless moments,
we discover each other
vein by vein.

Peel, embrace, undress.
Find skin, chest,
a heart, its beat within.

On snow days without wind or rain
we discover each other, again.

No solace from rain
(after 'Name' by Carol Anne Duffy)

When we were born, when your name
was found in shadow, that noun,
your voice, rose in me like a charm.

Did you hear me call? My vowels
echoed like sunrays on morning jewels.
The tips of our kisses, the breath

of our lips, were consonants
tying us together. Your mouth
was a channel, its touch, a kiss.

I travelled your words. Explored your name
exploded it, discovered it again
plagued by its rumble. Rain

caresses my hands on your hair. It
is like silk. I kiss an alphabet
of spells, or a curse. I wish

away your witching. It
resembles poison, like madness, like night
or an old hags grin. No light

enters this crumbling tower. Re-name
this venom a viper's kiss. My rhyming
heart is done. You inhabit my everything.

Truth

Somewhere between heron and tern
where cedar dances by an empty shore
we witness a floating coracle;
it labours uncannily off the sand. You pray
for its bowl, its frame of bone and skin.
Tread towards its traveller's heart,
layering its path with marram grass.

Each morning we listen for the nomad sea.
You fear it's broken by giant waves.
We nourish it.
Feed our natures on salt and spray.
Our truths are prayers absorbed by shells
or pebbles washed in surf.

Beginning

Here between waves and shoreline
a swallow dips and curves.
You remember your first breath,
a fury of sun on your back,
an ocean in flurry as it meets a storm.

Did you balance in those hands?
Feel their tightness around your flesh?
Your separation marked by granite.
You curve back again
and again,
reach for a cedar's shade,
curl your fingers across a turtle's skin.

In this bowl of sand and sea
you search pilgrim tides for coral shells.
Your truth becomes a pendulum that taps
between stillness and surge,
waiting for surf to fall.

Hope

In these shells, fragile truths, our prayers
lie in shallows – alone, unanswered – in worship
of the tide. Questions tease among each wave's
pull and drag – as shells merge into shingle, as water revives,
as cedar keeps its shade. In this sway of sand and sea
we mingle in the spray, pause between shore breaks,
anticipate each tempest; delay each fall, each footprint.
We welcome every golden wave broken by oceans' depths;
luminous, they shimmer along the shore;
release banks of foam and salt. Remind us
how blood and water engulfed our new-born selves.

Walking with ice

There's ice on the barbed wire.
Soil compressed on banks.
The *Chasse* search slopes for the dead
and not-yet-dead. Hunters ring warning bells
as they crawl, claw and tear, noses deep in bracken.
A stream coils frozen inside me, twisting
in snake-like movements.
I stop dead still. Nothing has changed,
yet everything has; light, silence, space.
Two deer, white speckled necks, graze the roadside.
They straighten, listen, leap in single bounds
above the snapping ice.

Bringing home the bread

This crescent morning, so dim it fades to light blue.
So cold it reaches deep into memories
of whispers, locker rooms, wet anoraks;
longing for chocolate and letters from home
or smiles that deadened the damp.
But now, drawing curtains, pulling on extra socks,
and mud-coated boots; a ritual of
hat, scarf, gloves before unlocking doors.
Testing the slip and slide of gravel.
The *chemin* in half dark, enough to fear goblins and wild boar.
Finding alterations. Evidence of fox holes through a bramble fence.
Fallen branches, a tree trunk pushed into a bank, an open gate.
Footprints of a phantom wild cat, of lion proportions.
To the top, behind a barbed wire barrier, the *Chasse* stalk.
Their dogs – all teeth and blood, drench the valley in choruses.
Here fields wake to green light reaching a pink horizon;
red chimneys are scattered like berries;
droplets of smoke fill the mammoth air.
Here, in a lamplit kitchen, eggs fry on a hob.
A radio plays *As Time Goes By*. Wounds are bound.
Confidences shared. Promises are as treasured
as the warmth of baked bread.

It is enough
(after 'Digging 1' by Edward Thomas)

What is the lesson of April? Could it be
the cuckoo's call a tempo for spring?

Can enough morning dew
bid goodbye to dust and ash?

Or banish woodsmoke beneath a chestnut's arms?
We crumble violets between our fingers

or lie among the bluebells growing
in the shade of new born earth.

Welcome dawn, a woodpecker drums,
beating shadows across a forest of butterflies.

Temper gentle winds, flush out the sad.
Let graylags fly before ice ravages our door again.

Journeying through

Up the *chemin*, touched by frost
on scrub, fences, stiles,
we follow footprints.
Shepherds, herders, hiders of children.
Their voices linger.
Fog hides their hillside, covers pines.
There are rose hips. A muck bucket by a horse's field.
Kites curve their gorge.
We climb beyond the dolmen,
look down on un-tucked fields,
silhouettes crowd the dusk.
Ice freezes our nostrils, fingertips
we must not linger.
It's still their time.

Morning crossing

One thousand feet once crossed our track,
past touching trees, over chestnut leaves.
A single heron flies north.
Blackened wings block all light,
bring shadow and shade between earth and cloud.
A foal runs, seeking her mother.
We slip on roots, tumble through foliage.
Raindrops fall from oaks under the beige sky.
We reach a barrier, ten foot high,
dank shrubs, unruly, untamed, untouched.
The sun hides behind morning's first fume.
We hear marching,
soft at first,
of one thousand feet crossing our track.

The night-time visitors of a dying country man

Aren't you curious the dying man cries from an open
window. Its latch scratches a wall of crumbling stone. He
scrapes black soil etched inside his palms, a life-line where
rivers once reached from finger to thumb. His unstilled hands
fall like damp moss. He's taunted by dreams; a brown haired
shepherdess; *don't depart this night alone* she pleads; red
hooded daughters, lost on acorn paths. *Show me the darkness*,
he prays, *its secrets, its untold stories, a moon to guide my
children home*. No-one witnesses the log fire die, or catches
the hedgehog feeding her young. A red fox peers through
brambles, its eyes like embers. Morning unveils its amber
wings. A song thrush calls from the chestnut tree.

Awakening 1

I'm an oak door fixed to granite, hidden by ivy.
You will not find me. Weeds grow at my feet.
Apples rot. Rivers roar within me.
I block your riddles. Winter falls,
hides my ears, your words are ice.
Through me lies all I know. Knock
as you wish, you cannot enter.
I have no key.

Awakening 2

I slept one hundred years.
I hear you. Just. Your voice a feather.
You cannot trust the orchard rain.
Do you know my path home?
Your hands are cut.
There's light in your pain.
Unfurl my frozen fingers.
Dine with me. Feed me – rubies.

Shucking oysters

She teaches me to shuck oysters with a small wooden
spear. Pushes its sharp edge into the hinge, prises off the
lid. Cuts muscle. Pokes its lips to check it's alive. Her eyes
examine my work, my raw hands. I learn how to stab the
blade, remove particles of shell and blood left in pink and
grey flesh. We place mollusks garnished with lemons on
an oval platter. She mentions foxes seen at dawn. She fears
for lambs, their mother already dead. A wolf sighted on
the plateau leaves carcasses scattered across fields. A horse
tumbled into a ditch on Sunday. The tractor couldn't shift
it. A kite floats over meadows, calling her young.

Seaside observations

Two poodles parade the promenade, sculptured legs, their
top knots held high. They pose on an esplanade, runners pass,
chatting; a man scraps in rubble – an old pram, sofa springs,
wires, a toaster. Gulls cry from damp pavements, guard
bones and eggs shells. Sirens hurtle by. People in duffle coats
shop, pick up children, settle down to fish and chips. Mrs
Sloane pulls her bag up twenty steps. Switches on her kitchen
strip light, sits on her mother's old chair. Remembering. She
sings with the gas ring heating her soup. You've gone to buy
a hairdryer and cayenne pepper, climb the long hill near a
coffee shop. Ours. Beyond is a pebbled shore. A lone bather
walks into still slate shallows. Letting go in the waves, her
head becomes indistinguishable

Mother's gaze
(after The Big Sleep *by Raymond Chandler)*

Most nights she darned our stockings,
biting off thread with razor teeth.
I liked the way her feline frame leant,
her tawny hair falling over her face;
how she kissed my forehead; my nose
pressed deep into her perfumed neck.

She taught me to stave off predators,
cross my legs, leave passenger doors unlocked.
She taught me to stare, taut lipped, expressionless,
when dog mouths pushed into mine,
hands reaching everywhere

To me she was bright green with life, so durable.
Yet the hardest jerks rolled over on sight
of her porcelain skin.
To them she remained a puzzle,
impenetrable like a safety curtain.

How delicate, how small, they said
as she floated through blue spring air.
Eyes slate grey, lashes cuddling her cheeks.
Thinking was no longer her problem.

Instances of blue

Sunday morning we rise to kites scanning fields of birthing *Limousin*.
Heat rises above bushes ripe with blackberries.
Branches of oak and chestnut reach across a strip of water,
leaves fondle electricity lines.
You swim circles of a pond
dark trees shadow your head.

Your thoughts wrestle with moments in Regent's Park –
a band played *Layla*.
A picnic hamper, champagne flutes.
There were no clouds, sky without threat of rain.
Somewhere a peacock cried.
That kiss.

We shelter in a covered café,
A tartan blanket hugs your shoulders.
A phone rings
blue algae in the river, someone shouts.
Grey clouds gather.
A tractor passes with a trailer of calves,
metal tags stapled to their ears.
Butterflies mingle in lavender.
We wait for news.

Green Ribbon

After the roof comes down
when seasons change
before a blaze controls your yellow voice
words bleed
in silence.
Each burnt breath crawls   through sand
fleeing ashes.
Nothing's left in this burning house
but bones
beneath clothed rubble
where your essence remains
untamed.

Crossing the line

That summer, when mother locked herself in her room,
father, you wept
into a folded silk handkerchief, taken from your breast-pocket.
At night you'd slip bible verses under my door.
Instructed me to learn them
by heart.
Children obey your parents in the Lord.
Often, I would find you staring from your study window.
Bible opened at Exodus, flat against your blotter.
Mother fox-trotted overhead.
I wrote you letters, underlining words:
beguile, beseech, forgive,
behead.
Then lit each one, burnt for eternity.
Father, you wept
when mother returned to the breakfast table.
Her hair in Carmen Rollers, arms in red silk gloves.

The falling of Gibson's mother

Her death is dark blue. A petrol sky. Beyond the moor. By
a river, swollen, overflowing, splitting trees in its path. Her
sleeve caught in branches. Her hands clutch her womb.
Who heard her fall? There are candles. Music. Happy
New Year. A fiddle, laughter, clapping, brethren dance in
feverish steps. A fire burns, its flames scar the heavens.
A rocket splits its gunpowder across the black; lighting
gargoyles, a church spire, a bent cross. Shouts thunder
with each flare. Here an apple bobbing, a chocolate pear,
a pocket full of sweets. Hands steady a baby swaddled in
lambswool. Someone flings a coin. Heads or tails? Auld
Lang Syne and a ceilidh into the morning hour. Day
brings its sapphire truth. Softly she floats.

On receiving a brooch on her wedding day
October 1946

London froze that October. Post-war wedding bells rang
across Chelsea. Faces stared from pictures. Many she never
knew. Just a few at her nuptials. Smiles caught on camera,
on a rainy day. A grey-eyed ghost gave her a brooch. She'd
heard the stories from her mother. Someone begat someone
else, and so it went on (as did the butchering). Even now she
wonders at its power. Then a night train, a coastline. Walks
through heather. A river, stone bridges. Searching for its
home. She, a trespasser, heard those faraway voices hidden
in sand and salt; *Atonement*. She tossed the brooch into the
spray.

Grief
(*after* To the Lighthouse *by Virginia Woolf*)

For a moment one word engulfs this house.
It hovers over stairs,
creeps through key holes,
swallows milk jugs,
pudding basins,
bowls of peaches and apricots.
It seeps into bedrooms, around curtain poles,
inspects a sailor's box.
It calls your name, earnestly.
Laughs at your faux-pas.
It breathes a hundred hurried syllables,
misheard, misfired.
It breaks locks, slams doors, builds a temple
in your memory.
It retires when midnight chimes.
Leaving a thousand lost sentences.

Missing signs

At dawn a green woodpecker sings,
hidden within a fog of wood
amongst brown bracken
and blackberry brambles. He laughs
amid its leaflessness, its bare souled oaks.
In that place where life is sheltered under soil,
undented by hoarfrost – he calls
I am here.
He overcomes his desire to sleep –
but heralds April, lets nature rest.
Or does he mock us?
Our hands and heads encased in wool,
we walk in half dark, missing
webs of snow that magic the world alive.

About the author

THE AUTHOR, Kate Rose, writes from her home in the Creuse, France. Her chapbook *Brushstrokes* was published by Mosaïque Press in May 2022. Her work has been reproduced in a range of collaborative anthologies and on-line publications. Her poetry has been published in Italian and Romanian in bilingual anthologies supported by the University of Salerno and West University of Timisoara respectively. She is co-founder of Artemesia Arts, with whom she hosts an annual poetry weekend, poetry@treignac.

Meet her at *www.katerose.online* and *www.artemesia-arts.com*

About the illustrator

COVER ILLUSTRATOR Nia MacKeown is a Pembrokeshire-born artist with a passion for painting *en plein air*. A member of the Royal Institute of Oil Painters (ROI), she has been a full-time professional artist since 2016, painting the things she loves, mainly in oils: imagery of everyday life, of the endearing commonplace, and landscapes tempered with reflection and light.

Her work has been shown at the ROI exhibition, the New English Art Club, the Royal West Academy exhibition, the Wales Contemporary, and the Artist Magazine open exhibition.

She lives with her husband and two small children in Cardiff.

To view her portfolio, visit
www.niamackeown.co.uk